J 616 .858 842 Pet

Pettenuzzo, B.
I have Down's syndrome.

387226

PRICE: $16.50 (90/m)

J
616
.858
842
Pet

Pettenuzzo, Brenda.
   I have Down's syndrome : Brenda Pettenuzzo meets
Helen Jayne Anderson / [Brenda Pettenuzzo] ;
photography, Maggie Murray ; consultant, Down's
Syndrome Association. -- London ; Toronto : F. Watts,
c1987.
   32 p. : ill. -- (One world)

"Handi-read."
Includes index.
03843793 ISBN:0863135722

(SEE NEXT CARD)

11329   89AUG21   90/m   1-00931243

OCT - 1989

I have
DOWN'S SYNDROME

I have
DOWN'S SYNDROME

Brenda Pettenuzzo
meets
Helen Jayne Anderson

Photography: Maggie Murray

Consultant:
Down's Syndrome Association

FRANKLIN WATTS
London/New York/Sydney/Toronto

Helen Jayne Anderson is eleven years old. She has Down's Syndrome. She has one brother, David, aged six. Her father, Bill, is a minister in the Methodist Church and her mother, Olive, is a teacher. Helen and her family live in Mountsorrel, a village near Loughborough in Leicestershire.

Contents

© 1987 Franklin Watts
12a Golden Square
LONDON W1

ISBN: 0 86313 572 2

Series Consultant: Beverley Mathias
Editor: Jenny Wood
Designer: Edward Kinsey

Typesetting: Keyspools Ltd

Printed in Hong Kong

The Publishers,
Photographer and author
would like to thank Helen
Jayne Anderson and her
family for their great
help and co-operation in
the preparation of this
book.

Brenda Pettenuzzo is a
Science and Religious
Education Teacher at St
Angela's Ursuline Convent
School, a Comprehensive
School in the London
Borough of Newham.

The early years

"Although we live in Mountsorrel now, I wasn't born here."

When Helen was born, her father was still training to be a minister of religion. He was at college in Edgbaston and he and Helen's mum lived in Birmingham. It came as a shock to find that their first child had been born with Down's Syndrome. They were still quite young and, like most people, thought that only older parents had children with Down's Syndrome. They were lucky to have the support of many friends and relatives during the early weeks and months of Helen's life.

"While I was still quite small, my mum and dad heard about the Down's Babies Association."

The Down's Babies Association later became the Down's Children's Association, and is now called the Down's Syndrome Association. Its aim is to help people with Down's Syndrome achieve as much as they possibly can. Helen's parents heard about the Association after a doctor asked for some information leaflets to be sent to them. Through their contact with what is now the Down's Syndrome Association, Helen's parents met many other parents facing the same challenges. Helen's father is now the Chairman of the Down's Syndrome Association.

"The Down's Babies Association gave my parents lots of ideas about how to care for me."

Helen's mum and dad heard about a special course in Birmingham for parents like them, with handicapped children. Through this course they learned more about how children develop. They also found out the best ways to help Helen's development. As time passed, Helen began to make progress in just the same way as "ordinary" children do. Sometimes she was a little later in reaching certain milestones, but not very much so. Helen's parents decided that, as far as possible, they would treat her as a "normal" child.

**"While we still lived in Birmingham, I went to
nursery school. Then we moved to Wales and I went
to a new school."**

Helen first went with her mum to a Mothers and
Babies group, then to a playgroup. All this time her
parents were trying to keep her mind and body active.
Their aim was to help Helen achieve as much as
possible. When the family moved to Wales and her
dad started his work as a Methodist minister, Helen
joined the nursery class at a local school. Later on she
went to the infant school close to home. Helen
remembers these schools. She still has photos to
remind her of her early schooldays.

"When I was eight, we moved to Mountsorrel. Here things are quite different from Wales, but just as nice."

Helen and her family moved to Mountsorrel when her brother, David, was still quite small. Helen was old enough to understand the upheaval of moving house. She found it exciting to move to a new place, but she took with her many reminders of her old home in Wales.

At school

"Mum takes David and me to school and meets us afterwards. Our school is called Christchurch and St Peter's, and it's quite near our house."

Like many girls of her age, Helen knows her way to school and she has learned to cross the road safely. Lots of girls and boys with Down's Syndrome can be relied upon to make the journey to and from school each day. Helen's mum goes with her and David because he is still too young to go to school alone. Next year, Helen and David will no longer be at the same school. Helen will be old enough to go to secondary school.

"My class teacher is called Mr Gorton. There is also an extra helper called Mrs Neal. She often sits with me in class."

Mrs Neal is called an ancillary helper, and she is there to assist Helen with anything that the class might be doing. Helen does everything that her classmates do, but sometimes she does things a little more slowly. Helen has always enjoyed school, and since going to Christchurch and St Peter's she has made lots of progress. She has learned to read well, and continues to get better at all of the other skills which schoolchildren learn.

"Sometimes I work on my own, and sometimes I work with my friends. We do all sorts of things in my class."

Some children who have Down's Syndrome go to special schools, where all the children have special needs of one kind or another. Others, like Helen, are pupils at ordinary or "mainstream" schools. It is becoming more and more common for people like Helen to go to ordinary schools. This plan is more successful in some schools than in others. There are advantages and disadvantages to both systems. Helen is happy at her school. She gets lots of help and support, and her parents hope that she will go on to the mainstream comprehensive school next year.

"I do lots of interesting things which help me with my number work. I really like being in the shop."

Like most other children with Down's Syndrome, Helen is at a younger stage of development in many things than the others in her class. She is getting better all the time. Her parents and teachers do not assess her progress by comparing her with other children. They look at each new skill and ability which she acquires. Each one can be seen as a milestone on Helen's journey.

"David brings a packed lunch to school. He doesn't like school dinners, but I do."

Some children who have Down's Syndrome have feeding problems when they are small. Some find it hard to chew solid food, and others cannot digest certain foods easily. Helen did not have these problems, and she enjoys eating all sorts of foods. She likes the way that school dinners are organised. She knows exactly what to do. She likes to be able to sit with her friends and talk about the morning's work. After she has eaten her lunch, she can play in the playground with her friends.

"I've always liked water, ever since I was a baby. I go swimming with my class every week."

When she was quite small, Helen's parents discovered that she loved water, even if it was very cold. They encouraged her to learn to swim. Swimming is very good for her muscles. Many children with Down's Syndrome have muscles which are more "floppy" than those of ordinary children. Some children with Down's Syndrome have problems with exercise because they have heart defects. This may prevent them from doing strenuous things. Helen is lucky. Her heart and circulation are quite normal.

Our church

"My dad is the minister at our church, but he sometimes leads the service at other churches instead. I usually go to Sunday School first."

While the adults are at the first part of the Sunday service at Helen's church, the younger people attend the Sunday School. At first, Helen was very shy and didn't want to take part. Soon she got to know the others and they got to know her. Now she enjoys all the activities. She spends the first part of the session listening to a story and talking about it.

"My Sunday School teachers always have a game or an activity for us that has something to do with the story."

Sometimes Helen doesn't want to join in with an activity, and no one ever tries to make her do it. She usually enjoys whatever they happen to be doing. Her Sunday School teachers have learned how to explain things in the way that Helen will understand. Just as in ordinary school, Helen is making progress all the time.

"I like the singing at the main Sunday service. We always go into the church at the end of Sunday School, but sometimes I go to the whole service."

The young people go into the main church for the last part of the service. If Helen's mum or dad is leading the service at their church that week, she may decide to attend the whole service instead of going to Sunday School. Whatever happens, the minister is careful to include the young people in the final part of the service. Helen is very fond of many of the hymns. She always joins in enthusiastically.

"After the service, lots of people stay behind for a chat at the coffee bar."

Many of the congregation stay for coffee or tea after the service. Nearly all of them know Helen, and she likes to speak to them. Helen has lots of friends in the church and in the local community. This has been a source of strength and support for her parents. They, in turn, have tried to pass on that strength to other parents whom they have met. Both Helen's mum and her dad are often asked to give talks to local groups about Down's Syndrome.

At home

"I have all sorts of games in my bedroom. When I was younger, my mum and dad played games with me a lot. Now my friends play as well."

Helen and David each have their own room, with their own favourite toys. Helen has lots of games. Helen's parents have always encouraged her to play with dominoes, jigsaws and similar games. This may have helped her develop many skills such as recognising colours and shapes. Just as with all young children, learning and playing are often the same thing.

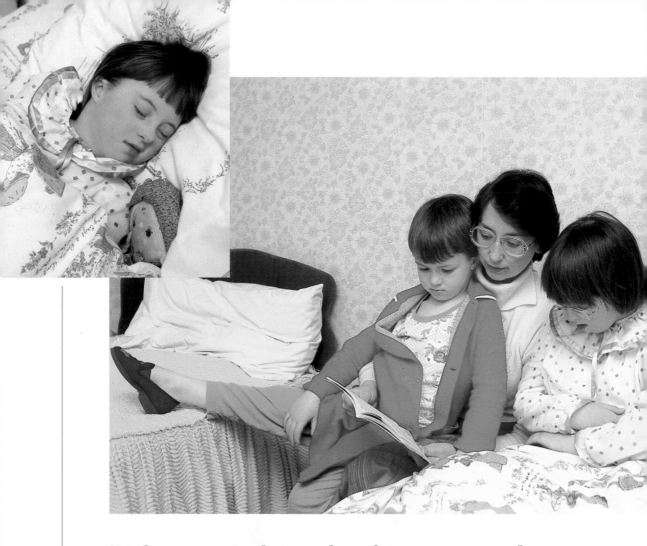

"Before we go to sleep each night, my mum reads a story to David and me. I mustn't forget to take off my glasses before I fall asleep!"

Although Helen has Down's Syndrome and David does not, in many ways they are just as similar as any other brother and sister. They both enjoy a story before they go to sleep, but they don't always agree over which story it's going to be. Helen keeps her glasses on until the very last minute. They are very important to her because, like many people with Down's Syndrome, she is quite short-sighted.

"I like playing games with my dad. Sometimes he forgets the rules and I have to remind him."

Helen's dad is a Methodist minister. This means that he works at their house quite often, because it is next to their church. It also means that he doesn't work ordinary hours. People often phone him up or ask him to go out at unusual times. He always makes time to be with both of his children and he plays lots of games with Helen. She always talks to him about what she has been doing at school and with her friends.

"Our dog is called Daisy. She takes us for lots of long walks! We have a cat as well."

Not far from Helen's home, there are several nice places for walking. Whenever the weather and work allow, the whole family goes out for walks at the local beauty spots. Like many people with Down's Syndrome, Helen's skin tends to be dry and get chapped easily, and she isn't as sensitive to changes in temperature as other children of her age. When they go out for a long walk, her parents make sure that she doesn't get too chilled or that she doesn't overheat. Sometimes, when they get home, she takes much longer than David to cool down.

"My mum lets me help cook the dinner. I like making custard."

A few years ago, many people thought that children with Down's Syndrome were unable to do many things. Now we know that there is a wide range of skills which can be learned by many people with Down's Syndrome. Helen's parents try to include her in all sorts of family activities. She enjoys helping around the house and in the garden, and she makes delicious custard!

"Meal-times in our house are nice times. We can all sit down together and talk about what each of us has been doing."

Helen's parents try to make sure that at least once each day the whole family sits down to eat together. When Helen was born and her parents learned that she had Down's Syndrome, they were shocked and upset at first. Later they realised that Helen was to be a challenge to them. She is a valuable member of society, and her parents, with their relatives and friends, are trying to make sure that she leads as happy and as fulfilled a life as she possibly can.

Facts about Down's Syndrome

Down's Syndrome gets its name from Doctor Langdon Down. In 1866 he identified a set of characteristics and symptoms which certain mentally handicapped children seemed to have in common. At first he associated only about twelve characteristics with the condition, all of them things which he had observed. As medical science has allowed more complex investigations to be done, the number of clinical signs of Down's Syndrome has increased. Most medical textbooks identify over fifty signs, and there have been studies which have listed up to 300. Most of these signs are uncommon and have little effect upon the child's growth and development.

Each year in England and Wales about 700 babies are born with Down's Syndrome (around 7.3 per 10,000 births.) There does not appear to be any regional variation, and the overall numbers do not seem to change much over a ten year period. The greatest number of Down's Syndrome babies is born to mothers aged less than 35 years, since this is the age group of greatest child-bearing. However, when the birth-rate of Down's Syndrome babies to mothers of different age groups is compared, it is seen that there is a much greater likelihood of it happening to the babies of older mothers. Over a five year period, the numbers of Down's Syndrome babies born to women range from about 1 in 2,000 live births for women aged under thirty years to more than 1 in 125 live births for women aged over forty. Down's syndrome is found in all races, all social classes and all countries of the world. No connection has yet been established between the condition and diet, illness, geographic region or climate.

Most newborn babies with Down's Syndrome can be recognised by their slightly slanted eyes and the extra fold of skin on the inner side of each eye. Many have a smaller than average head and the back of the head tends to be flattened. They are often found to have small, low set ears, and sometimes the tops of the ears are folded over. The mouth looks small, and inside there is less space, so that the tongue tends to stick out. This is made more noticeable by the fact that the children have more floppy muscles than average, so the mouth is often open. There is also a broadness in the hands and feet, and sometimes unusual creases in the hands and feet. Many newborn babies with Down's

Syndrome do not have all of these signs, but most of them have several of them. In addition there are many other characteristics which are present to a greater or lesser extent. Most of the differences in appearance are due to the unusual development of the skull and the rest of the skeleton, which also affect the eyesight, hearing and breathing. The babies do not grow at the same rate as ordinary children, and most children and young adults look younger than they really are because of this. By four to six years they are on average about 13cm, shorter than ordinary children. The average young man with Down's Syndrome is likely to be between 145cm and 168cm tall and the average young woman a few centimetres shorter at 132cm to 155cm. There are, however, plenty of exceptions who fall within the normal ranges for height and build.

Babies and children with Down's Syndrome often have skin which appears different to that of other children. It can be unusually dry, and have poor circulation which makes it appear 'marbled.'

About 30 to 40 percent of babies born with Down's Syndrome may have some type of heart or circulatory defect. Many of these are very slight and some disappear during the early years of life. Only a few babies in every hundred suffer from a serious heart defect and most of these are treated by surgery as babies. Recent advances in surgery have meant that all children, including those with Down's Syndrome, have a much greater chance of surviving this sort of operation than used to be the case a few years ago.

There are many other ways in which babies, children and adults with Down's Syndrome differ from others, but in all these aspects there is a very wide range of what is considered 'normal' and in many cases, the range found in Down's Syndrome overlaps with the 'normal' by a wide margin.

In the 1950s scientists discovered the mechanism by which characteristics are passed on from one generation to the next. This led to an understanding of the true nature of Down's Syndrome. All living cells contain within their nucleus the 'blueprint' not only for that cell but for the whole organism of which that cell is a part. The blueprint is held in a chemical code in the molecules of a substance called D.N.A. This forms long strings called Chromosomes, and each type of living thing has a characteristic number of chromosomes in each of its cells, except for its reproductive cells. These contain only half the number so that when a male and a female cell are joined together (from the same species) their chromosomes are added together to form the proper number. Human beings have 46 chromosomes in each cell. These form 23 matched pairs, including two which determine whether the person is male or female. Scientists have been able to examine and photograph the chromosomes, and each pair has been given a number (except the sex chromosomes which are called X and Y). People who have Down's Syndrome have an extra chromosome number 21. This extra chromosome is usually separate from its partners, but in about 5% of children it is attached to another chromosome.

Each Chromosome is divided into sections called Genes, and there are genes which control every feature and characteristic of each organism. The extra genetic material inherited by people with Down's Syndrome is responsible for the differences in their appearance and development. However, people who have Down's Syndrome also have all of the other genes which they should have, so they have a great deal in common with their families as well as with other people with Down's Syndrome!

There are several ways in which the extra chromosome can occur in Down's Syndrome. In most cases it happens completely by chance during the production of eggs and sperms or during the first cell division after fertilisation. In a very few cases, one parent is a 'carrier' for the condition. They do not have an extra chromosome 21 but they have one which is wrongly placed. This is passed on with a normal chromosome 21 to produce a child with an extra one.

No particular cause has yet been found which explains the appearance of the extra chromosome. In about 20% of cases the extra chromosome has come from the father. In recent years many researchers have concentrated on finding ways of helping people with Down's Syndrome to achieve their fullest potential. Like all babies and children, those with Down's Syndrome respond to stimulation and attention from those about them. In many families development guidelines, and 'schedules' and games are used. These have helped the children to achieve far more satisfaction out of life and acquire more skills than would otherwise have been possible. There is a vast range of ability and achievement amongst people with Down's Syndrome. Thanks to recent developments in medicine and education, and changes in the attitude of the general public to those who are not 'ordinary' or 'average' far more than ever before will soon be able to lead happy, independent and fulfilled lives.

THE DOWN'S SYNDROME ASSOCIATION

The D.S.A. is the leading organization for helping parents and professionals with the care, treatment and training of children with Down's Syndrome. It has an expanding network of branches and support groups. At present there are thirteen branches in Britain and about 100 local groups. All branches are run by volunteers and provide objective and practical advice and information.

The D.S.A. underwrites specific projects which offer clear benefit to children and adults with Down's Syndrome. An educational research centre is operated by the D.S.A. at Birmingham Polytechnic.

Underpinning all the activities of the D.S.A is a resource library, based in London, which includes practical and audio-visual material as an aid to information and learning.

The D.S.A. is a registered charity which relies to a great extent on donations from business, trusts and individuals.

Details of all D.S.A. services and literature are available from:
The Down's Syndrome Association
12/13 Clapham Common,
Southside
London SW4 7AA
Tel: 01-720 0008

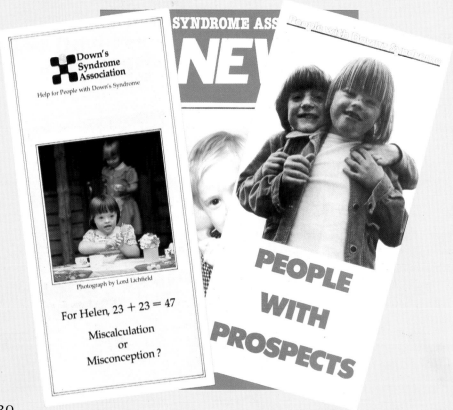

Glossary

Chromosomes Thread-like structures found within the nuclei of cells. Human cells contain 46. Each chromosome consists of D.N.A. and carries part of the blueprint for making a copy of the organism.

D.N.A. The abbreviated form for a chemical called Deoxyribosenucleic acid. This substance is not like familiar chemicals. Its molecular structure is very complex, containing hundreds of thousands of atoms. The way in which these atoms are arranged determines the exact function of each part of the D.N.A molecule.

Fertilisation The process by which new life is started when a male sex-cell joins with a female sex-cell from the same species. Each one contains one of each pair of chromosomes, and by joining together they form a new cell with the full complement of chromosomes.

Gene A section of a chromosome which contains the instructions for one part or function of the organism. Most characteristics are controlled by pairs of genes, which may indicate either a dominant or a recessive form of that characteristic. (e.g. blue or brown eyes).

Mainstream school Any school which takes children without specific disabilities.

Molecule A group of atoms which are chemically bonded together and cannot be separated from one another by physical methods.

Nucleus The central part of most living cells. It contains the chromosomes and controls all of the activities of the cell. It is usually seen as a darker mass in the cell when viewed through a microscope.

Special School A school which takes children who have specific disabilities or problems, which make it desirable for them to be taught in a more sheltered environment.

Syndrome A collection of symptoms which are associated with the same condition. Many 'syndromes' are named after the doctor or scientist who first made the connection between them.

X & Y Chromosomes The two chromosomes which determine the sex of an individual. In humans, two Xs mean a female and an X and a Y means a male. Very little other information is carried on the Y chromosome, but there are some genes on the X.

Index